Terry 12 Eyes
Toby Glover©2023

enjoy :)

Toby

Once upon a rainforest, under a moonlit sky, a little pink-toed tarantula called Terry was born in the beautiful rainforest of Brazil. He had six lovely brown eyes, pretty pink toes on the end of his eight furry legs and a smile that stretched across his face like a happy string of spaghetti. Terry thanked his mum for bringing him into the world, gave her a big hug, then ate her for breakfast. Afterwards he set up home in Tall Tree, not far from Big Water, the magnificent River Amazon. When he finished weaving his web he had a little sleepy-sleep-sleep for about a week, and woke up on Saturday morning to the sound of his belly rumbling. He scuttled around his web looking for a tasty fly, or cricket, or grasshopper or anything, but his web was empty.

"This is a bit crazy-craze-craze!"

But this was the least of his problems…little did he realise that danger was just around the corner. Well rather, it was coiling up his tree! Terry was about to come face to face with Grebby the Yellow Anaconda, a deadly snake who didn't care for spiders very much. He didn't think it fair that these furry little pink-toed creatures should have eight legs, while Grebby, a beautiful elegant creature, should have none.

"Well, well, well," he hissed, peering down at Terry with his glassy green eyes, "what have we here?"

"Hola, I'm Terry Tarantula."

"Well Terry," hissed Grebby, his voice was soft and dangerous, like the sound of boiling acid, "I'm Grebby the Yellow Anaconda and I run things around here, I'm in charge, I'm the Boss. And I want my snake snack!"

"Snake snack?" frowned the confused tarantula.

"Yeah! Grebby likes his snake snack! One fat grasshopper every morning!"

"But I haven't caught any grasshoppers yet, in fact I haven't caught anything yet! I'm starving!"

"Because your web is a mess! It's full of holes!"

"Really?" frowned Terry, "So that's why I've not caught anything!"

"Yeah, well you better start soon, otherwise I'll have to find a different kind of snake snack," threatened Grebby, flicking out his fork tongue at a terrified Terry, "perhaps something hairier with pretty pink toes!"

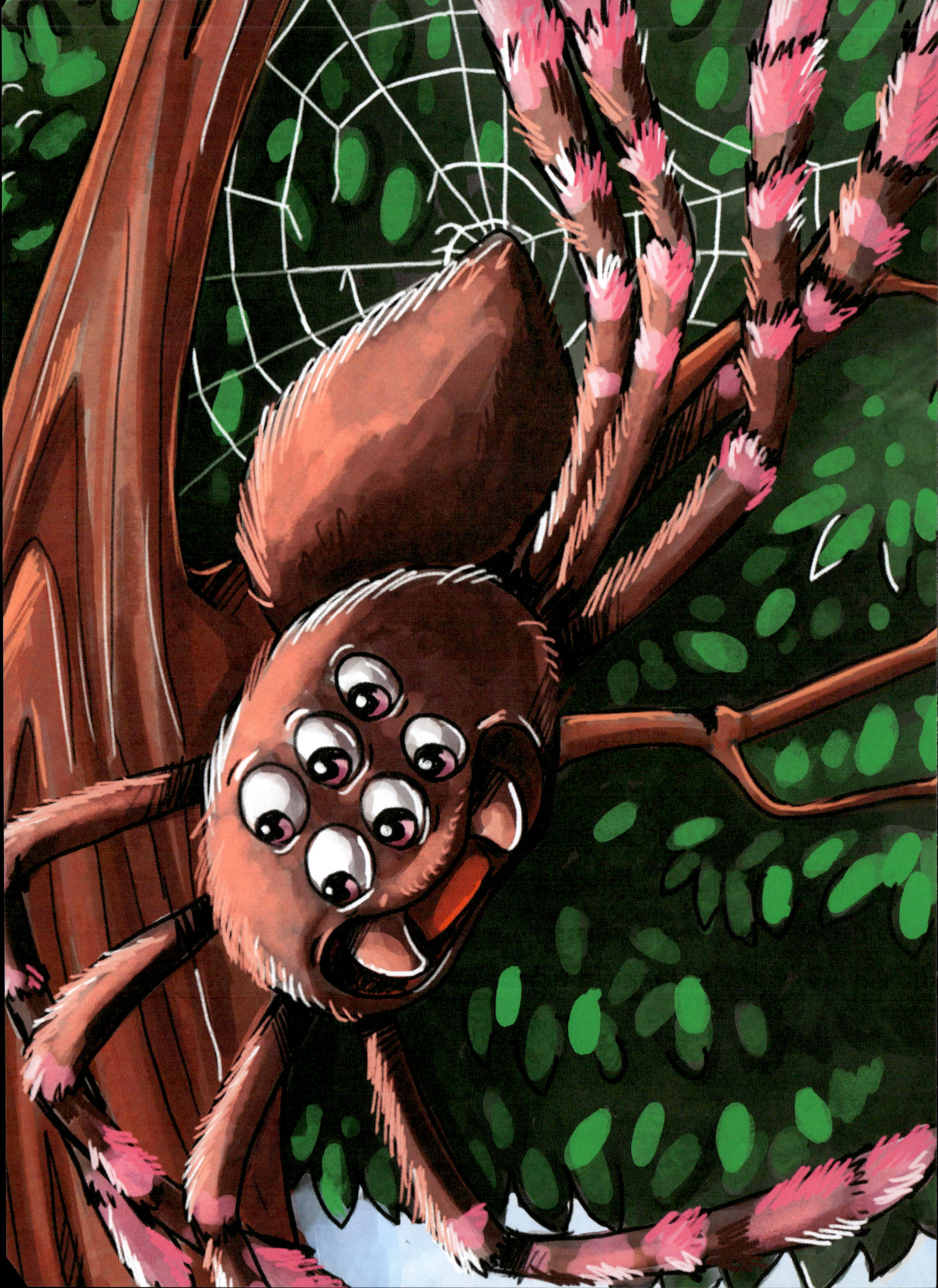

Terry watched him slither off then checked his web. He scuttled around the silky threads looking for gaps, but it all looked so blurry, he wasn't quite sure where he was going. By the time he finally came across a big hole, he fell right through it, landing at the bottom of Tall Tree with a dull PLOP!

When Terry regained consciousness he found himself lying on a scaly back.

"I fell out my tree!" he explained, "Ow! I can't feel my legs!"

"You'd best go see Doc Croc, he runs a surgery down by Big Water."

"Can you take me?"

"What do you think I am? Hmm? An ambulance? No chance! Besides, Doc Croc and I don't see eye to eye as it were," revealed Grebby, "Not since that thing last summer between me and his wife."

"What thing?"

"I ate her."

PLEASE WAIT

"Oh," gulped Terry and hobbled off to Doc Croc's surgery. He explained his dilemma to the monkey on reception, but because he didn't have an appointment she made him sit in the waiting room for a further two hours, squinting at out of date copies of HOLA! magazine.

"TERRY TARANTULA!" yelled the monkey eventually, "Doc Croc will see you now."

"Finally!" muttered Terry, hobbling down the hallway and knocking on a big door.

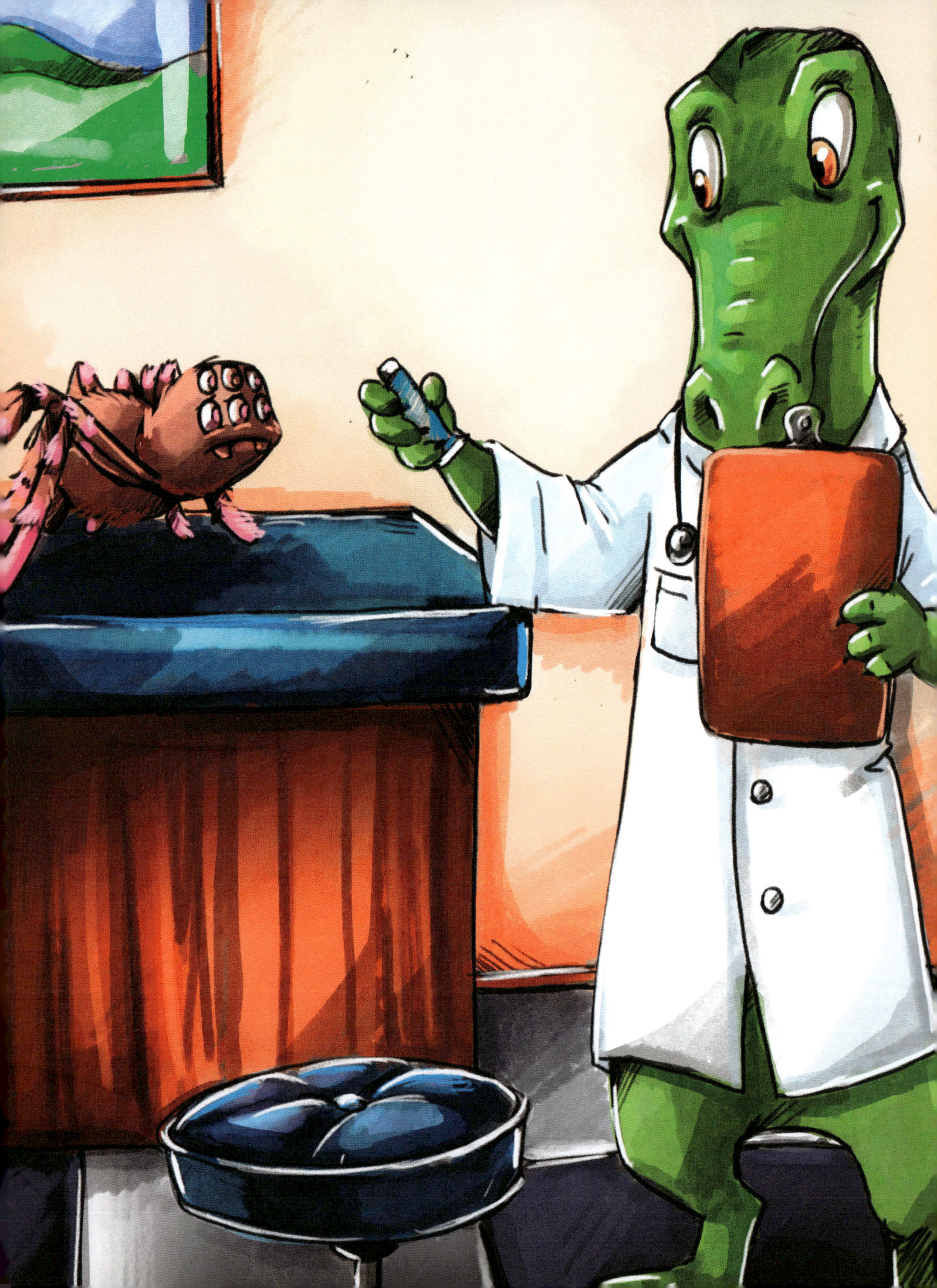

"Come in," called out Doc Croc, he had a deep voice, like he's talking to you from the bottom of a well, "now what seems to be the problem?"

"Hola, I fell out of my web," explained Terry, rather embarrassed, "and landed at the bottom of my tree and hurt my legs."

He heaved himself up from his chair and shuffled across to Terry. He was a huge creature but was getting old now and his legs ached wearily as they struggled to support his heavy frame.

"Yes, it looks like you'll have a sore bruise for a few days, I'll give you something to put on it."

Doc Croc began fishing about in his medicine cabinet, still chuckling away, "You know I still don't understand how on earth a tarantula falls out of his web?"

"I fell through a hole."

"A hole?"

"Yes, you see Grebby-"

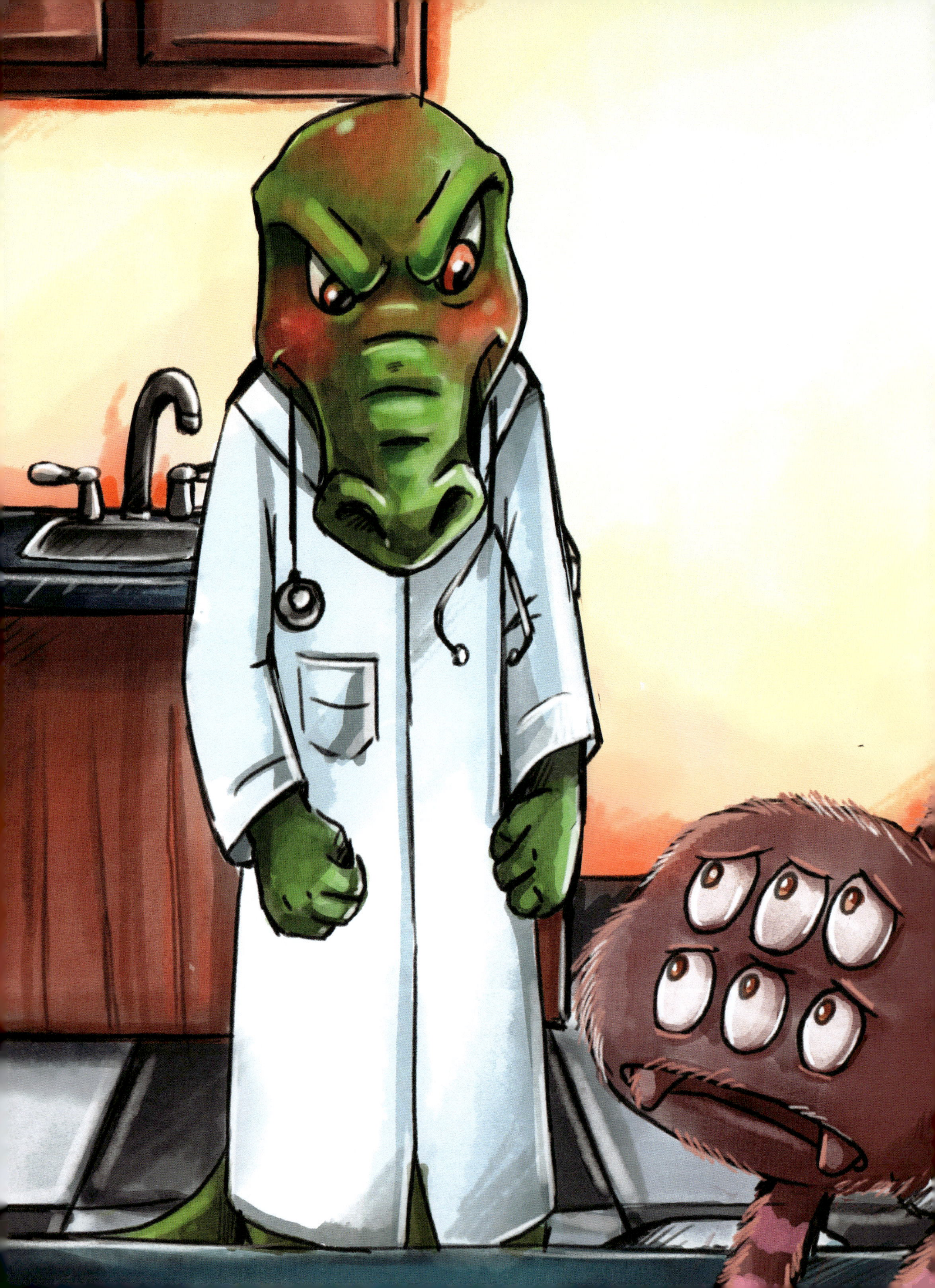

"NEVER EVER MENTION THAT NAME IN HERE!" BELLOWED Doc Croc, slamming his green scaly fist down hard on the medicine cabinet, scattering tablets everywhere.

Terry froze with fright, unable to continue. Doc Croc took some deep breaths and calmed down, but his face was still red with fury. "So, you were saying?"

"Well, er, yes, well," stammered Terry, choosing his words very carefully, "I was told by, er, somebody that my web was full of holes but when I tried to fix it I fell through one."

"That's strange," frowned Doc Croc handing over some lotion, "now follow the instructions on this bottle and you should be fine by the end of the week."

Terry squinted at the label, it was all blurry, "What does it say?"

"Can't you read yet?" frowned Doc Croc.

"I can read, but I can't see the words clearly."

E 1
F P 2
T O Z 3
L P E D 4
P E C F D 5
E D F C Z P 6
F E L O P Z D 7
D E F P O T E C 8
L E F O D P C T 9
F D P L N C E O 10

Doc Croc scratched his chin, "So you can't see the words and you couldn't see the holes in your web?"

"No," sighed Terry.

"My friend, I think I might know what the problem is, come and sit in this big chair and look at this chart."

Doc Croc took out his special eye testing equipment and asked Terry to try and read lots of different letters.

"Yes Terry, just as I thought! It seems you need glasses."

"Glasses?"

"Yes, spectacles," nodded Doc Croc, "you see Terry, your six eyes are very weak, so I need to make you some special lenses to magnify your eyesight and make it stronger. Then you'll be able to see better. Do you understand?"

Terry nodded and waited outside and had a little sleepy-sleep-sleep while Doc Croc used his special tools to craft some very important glasses.

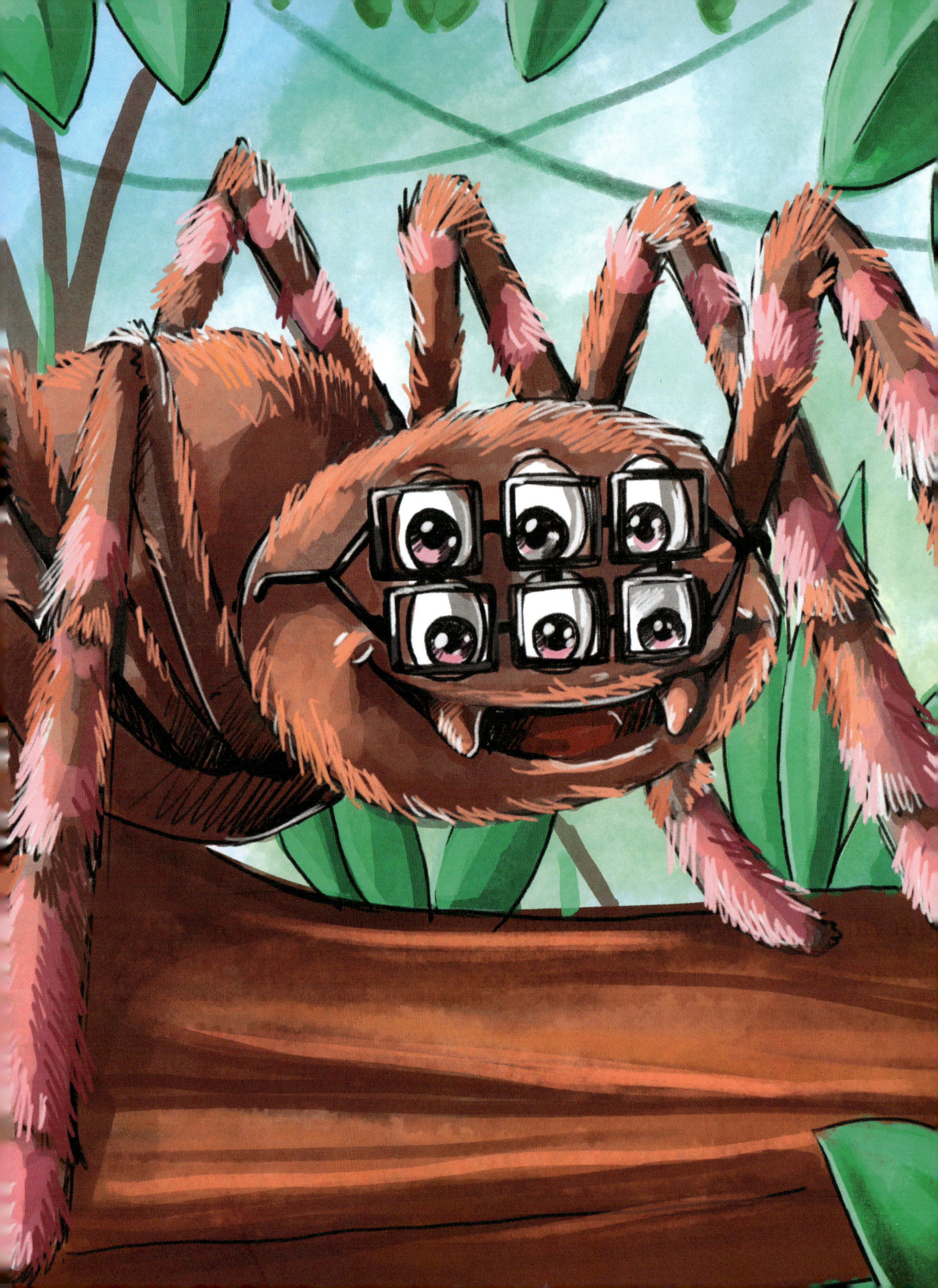

"Here you go," he announced proudly, sliding them onto Terry's head, "how does that feel?"

"WOW!" Terry couldn't believe his eyes! Everything was crystal clear, the rainforest was now awash with a rainbow of colours, sparkling waterfalls, beautiful flowers and pretty fluttering butterflies. Terry heard a swoosh and looked up to see the Blue Macaw, the biggest parrot in the world, swoop overhead in a blaze of amazing colour. For the first time Terry was able to appreciate fully the wonderful habitat in which he lived. He felt extremely lucky and very, very happy.

When he climbed Tall Tree, he was shocked to see how tatty his web had been all along. He'd just finished spinning some silk to fix it when the sound of horrid laughter startled him from below. Terry looked down to see Grebby staring up at him, laughing so much his sharp silver fangs were wobbling.

"Ha! Ha! Ha!" he hissed, "What are those things on your face?"

"My new glasses," answered Terry proudly.

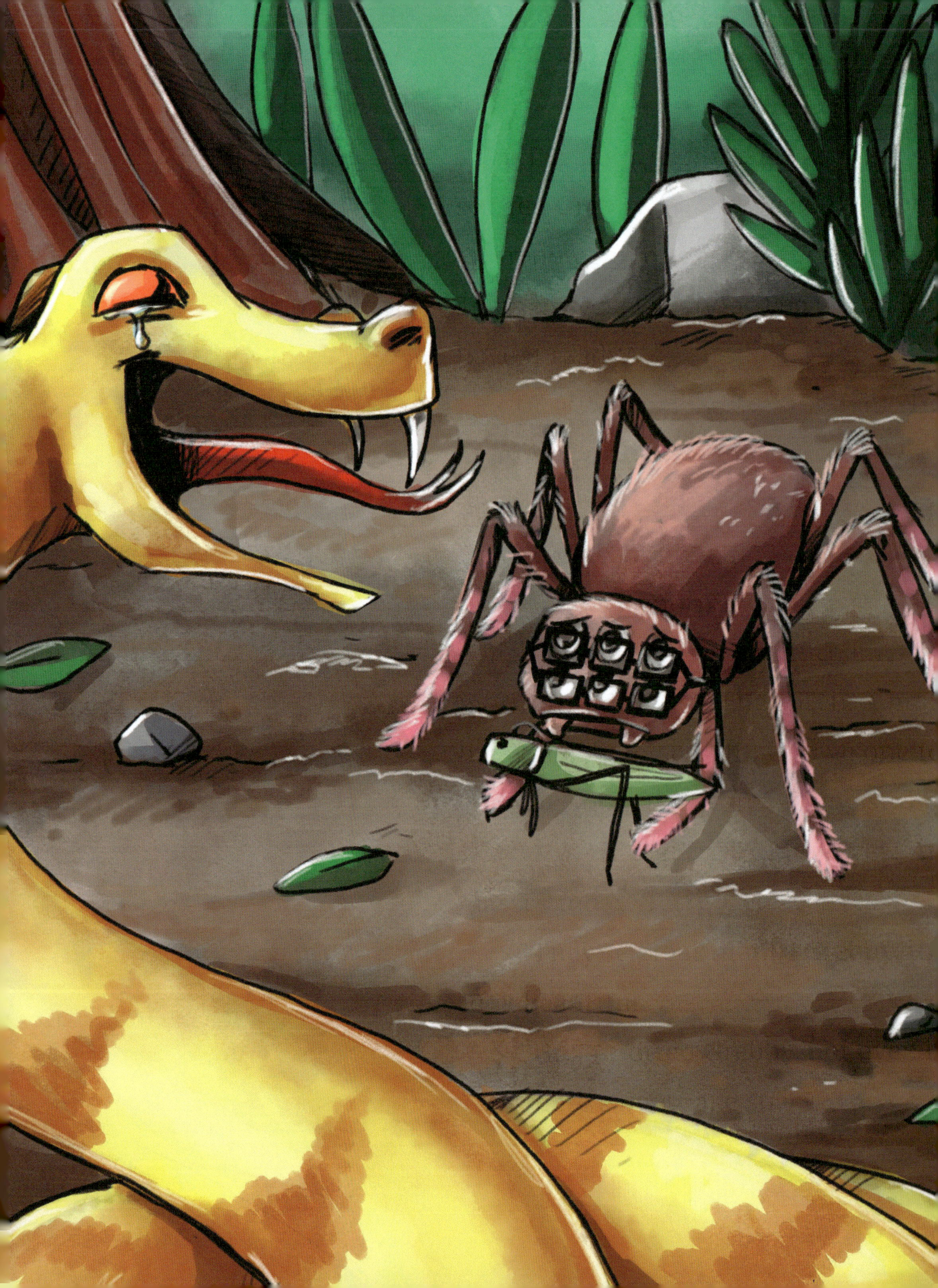

"I've never seen anything quite so ridiculous in all my life!" scoffed Grebby, "Ha! Now you've got twelve eyes instead of six! From now I'm calling you Terry Twelve-Eyes! Good day, Terry Twelve-Eyes! Oh and I'll be round for my grasshopper later, so have it ready."

Despite what Grebby thought, Terry was actually very happy with his new glasses, and took great care of them. That evening as the sun set low in the Brazilian sky, he took them off and placed them in his little case that Doc Croc had given him. The next morning, he cleaned the lenses, put them on, and delighted to discover two nice juicy grasshoppers and three fat moths trapped in the new web. A hungry Terry scoffed them for breakfast, being careful to save one for Grebby of course. Sure enough, soon afterwards, along slithered the yellow anaconda.

"Morning, Terry Twelve-Eyes! And how are your ridiculous glasses today, Terry Twelve-Eyes?"

"They're great thanks Grebby, they make your golden skin look beautiful."

"Ha!" snorted Grebby, not even bothering to say thank you, "So where's my snake snack?"

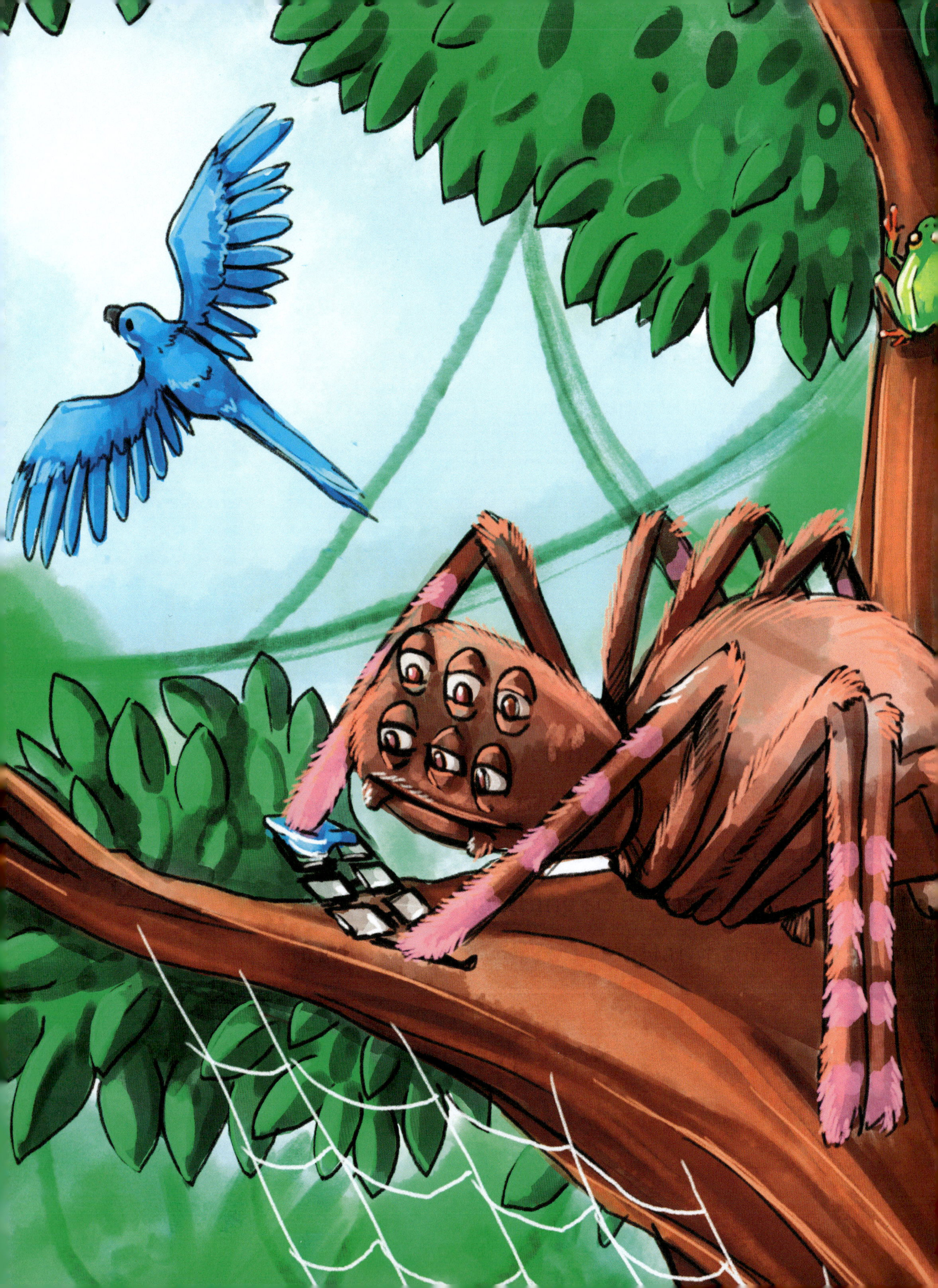

"Here's your snake snacky-snack-snack," smiled Terry, handing over the fat grasshopper.

"Finally!" hissed the Yellow Anaconda, once again not even bothering to say thank you, "I'll be back same time tomorrow. Good day, Terry Twelve-Eyes!"

Terry didn't really like being called Terry Twelve-Eyes but tried his best to ignore it. He didn't want to be nasty too by making up his own silly name for Grebby because Terry wasn't that sort of tarantula. He knew Grebby wished he had legs, but he never teased him about it, because he didn't want to upset him, and as we know, Terry wasn't like that.

And so, each morning Grebby would slither by, coil himself round Tall Tree and say, "Morning Terry Twelve Eyes! Where's my snake snack?"

To which Terry would simply reply with a tired smile, "Good Morning Grebby, here's your snake snacky-snack-snack."

But then, one sunny day, something awful happened…

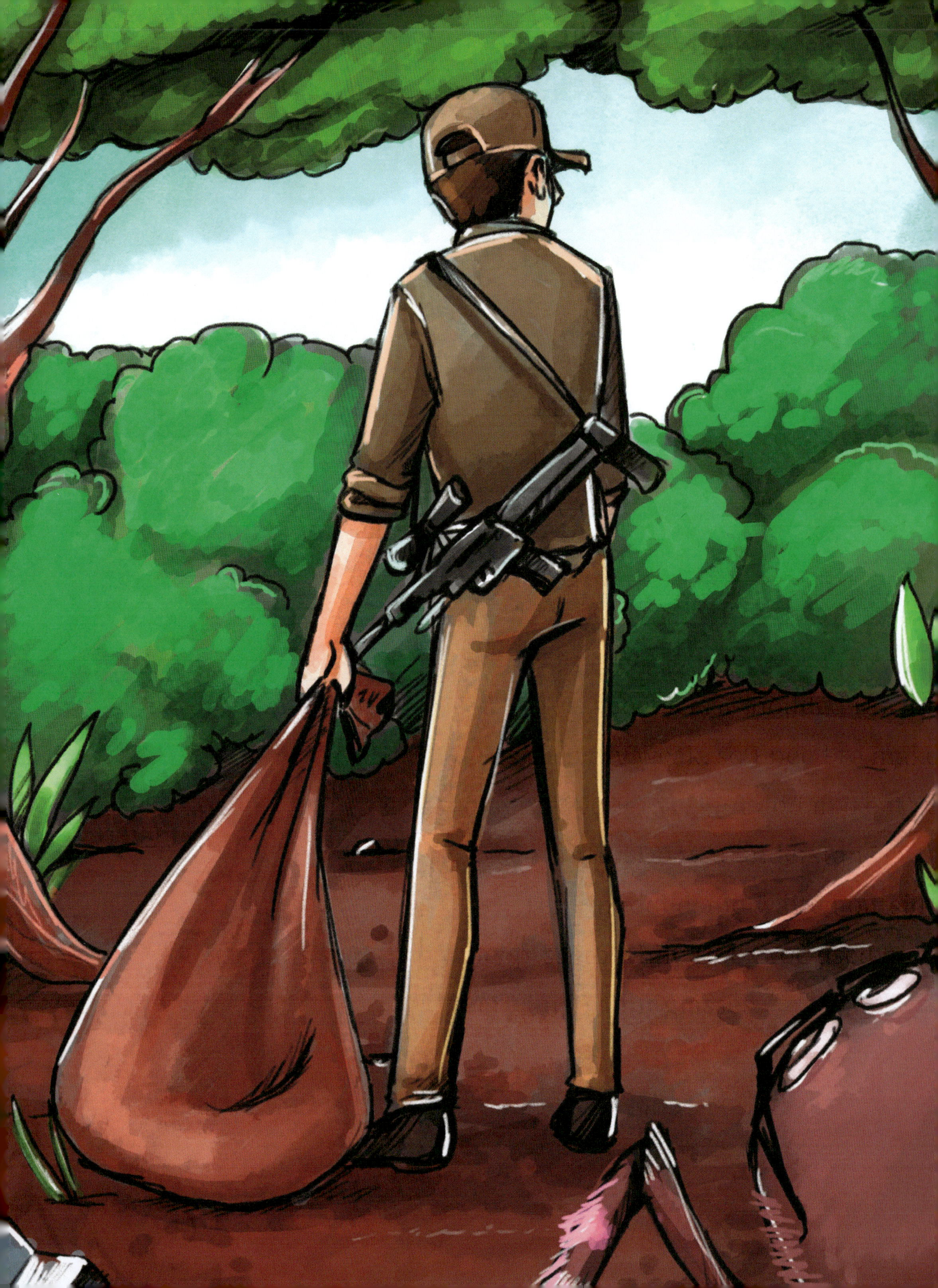

One morning Terry was brushing his teeth after a nice grasshopper breakfast, when he noticed the rainforest was strangely quiet. A few hours later Grebby still hadn't shown up for his snake snack and there was an odd atmosphere in the Amazon, so Terry decided to go and investigate. It was scorching hot and the sun shone high up in the bright Brazilian sky. Terry searched all morning but Grebby was nowhere to be seen. He was just about to give up and return to his web, when he saw something awful! Terry froze with fright, there before him stood the most dangerous creature in the rainforest.

A poacher!

By his side lay a large dark sack. Something long was trapped inside, thrashing about, but the end was tied with a thick knotted rope. The poacher held a big net in one hand and a tranquiliser gun in the other. Terry held his breath and hid in the tall grass, watching the poacher scan the rainforest for more animals to capture. Just then, he had a clever idea. He picked up a small rock and hurled it through the air. It made a rustling noise when it landed in the distant bushes and the poacher rushed over to investigate, his net held high above his head. As quick as a flash Terry sprinted over to the now unguarded sack, feeling very sorry for whatever was trapped inside.

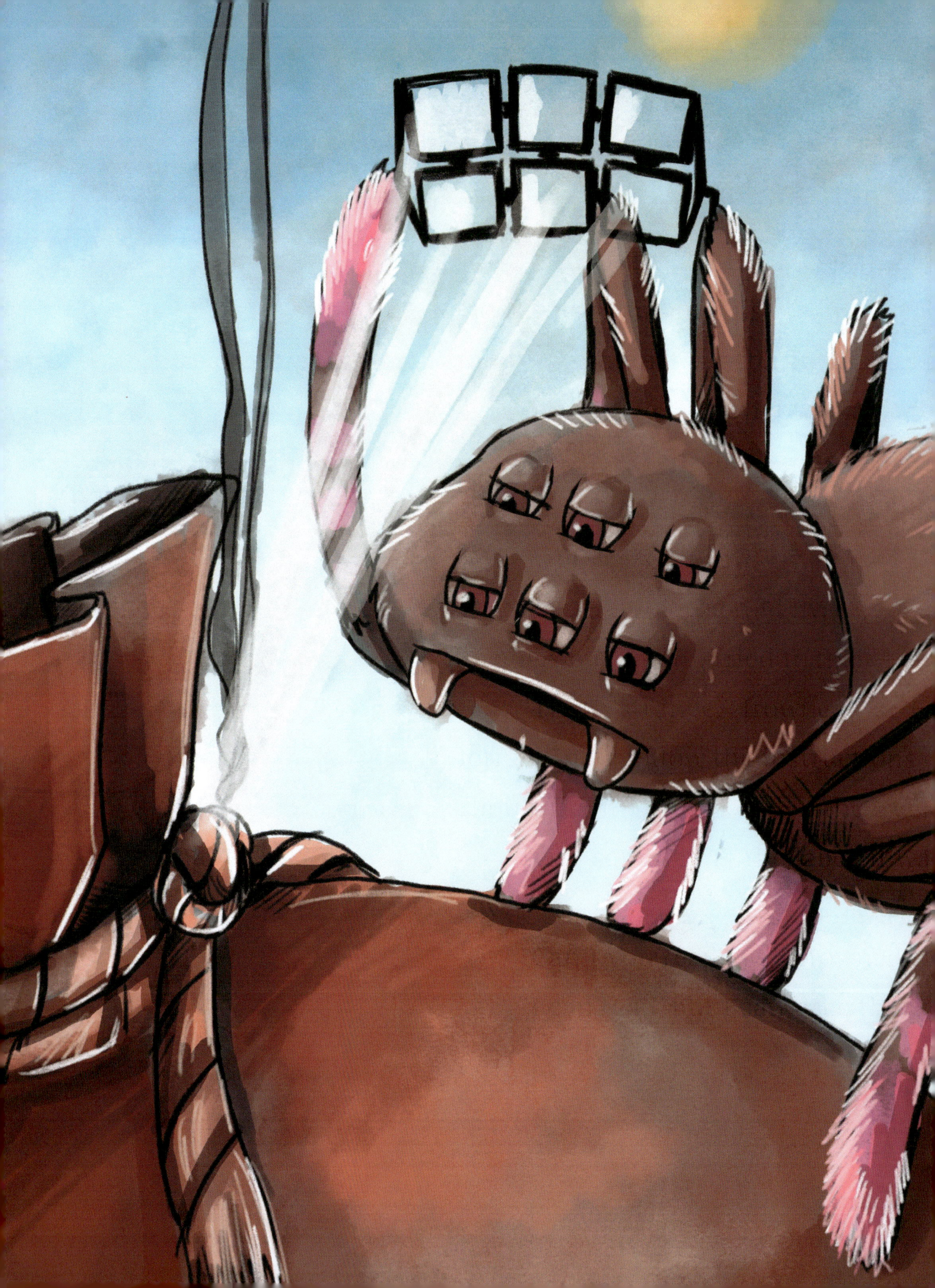

"Hola," he whispered, "are you okay in there?"

"Terry Twelve-Eyes!" came a sad sounding hiss, "Is that you?"

"Grebby! It's you!" gasped Terry, "I'll save you."

Terry crawled to the top of the bag and desperately tried to untie the rope. He yanked and pulled with all the mite in his eight legs, but it was no use, the knot was too tight. The snake was trapped! Unless Grebby was freed, he would die! The poacher would take him away, kill him, skin him and use his beautiful golden skin to make handbags, belts and shoes to sell to tourists. It was a terrible predicament! Just then Terry had his second clever idea of the day.

He remembered how Doc Croc explained that his special lenses magnified his eyesight by making it stronger. Maybe if Terry held his glasses up to the bright shining sun they could magnify the sunrays too? He took them off and held them up to the sun. Sure enough the sunrays shone through the lenses, creating a powerful hot beam which the clever spider aimed at the big knot.

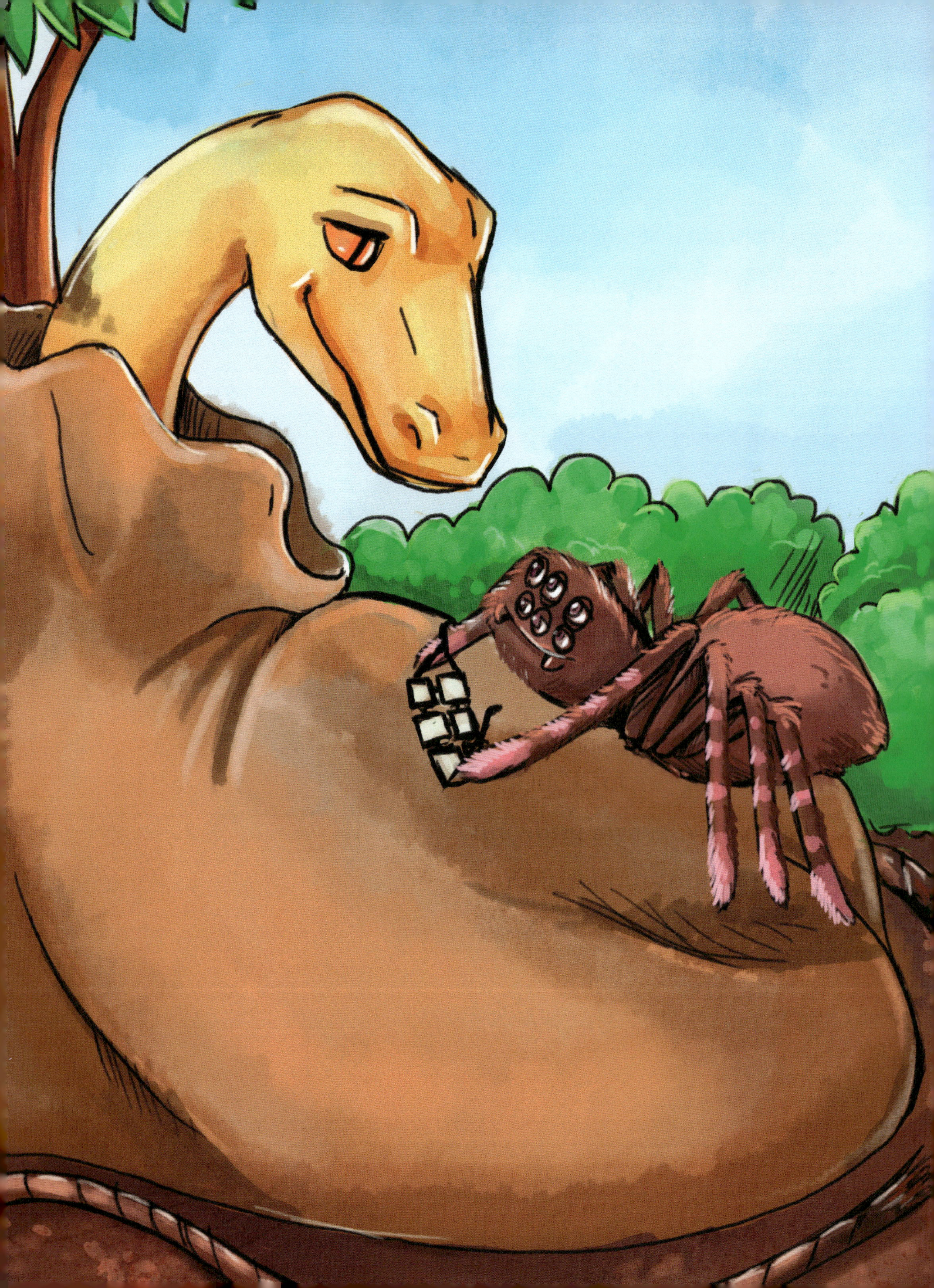

After just a few seconds the rope began to smoke, then burn, then SNAP! Grebby spilled out on to the tall grass, free at last!

"Oh thank you Terry Twelve-" but suddenly Grebby stopped, then corrected himself, "I mean, thank you Terry Tarantula!"

"My pleasure," he smiled, "I guess my glasses aren't so silly after all."

"No they're brilliant!" agreed Grebby, "Now let's get out of here!"

Soon they were both back to the safety of Tall Tree and everything was fine.

But then, something else dreadful happened…

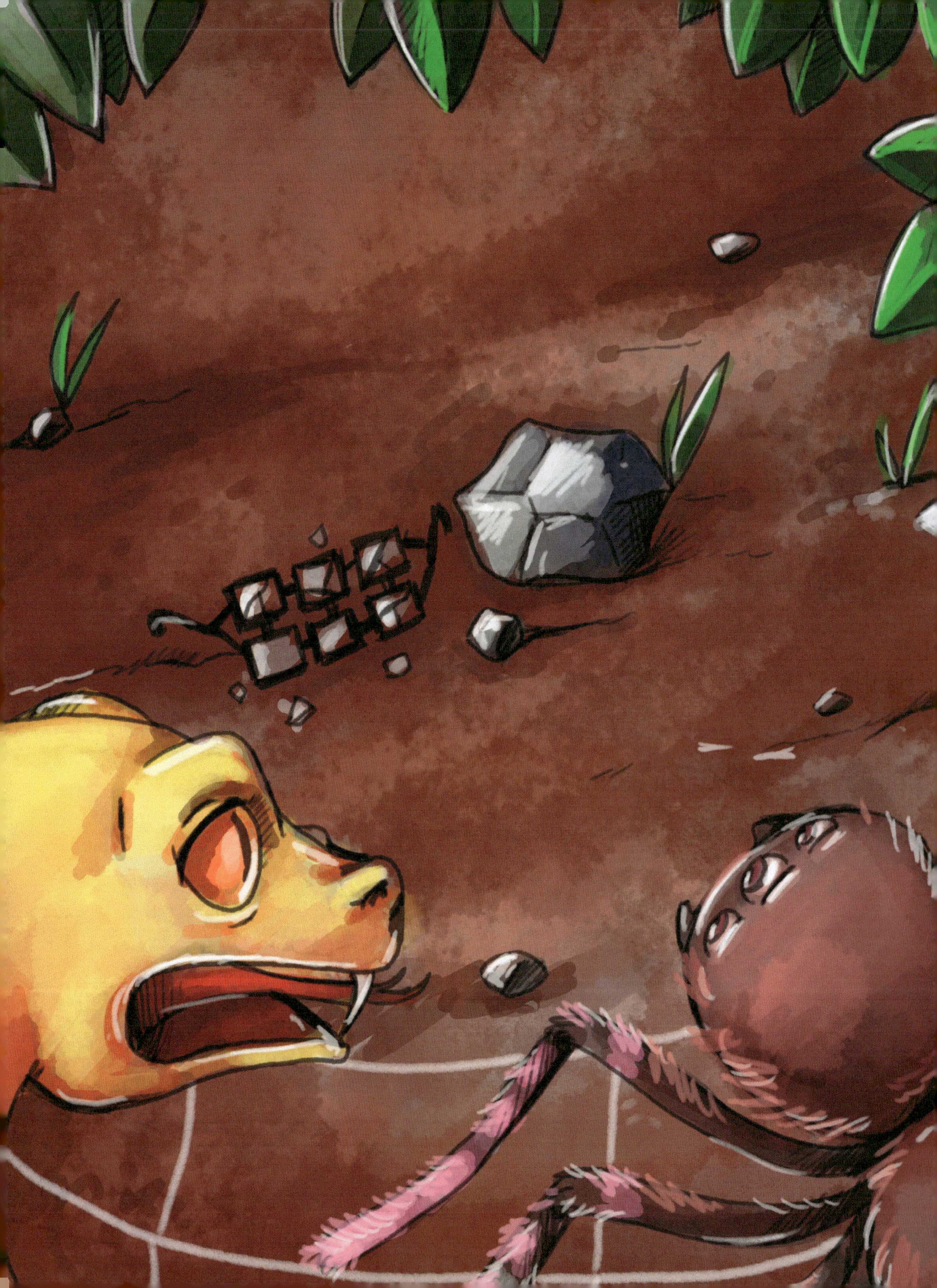

When Terry settled into his web and put his glasses back on, they were still so hot from the sun that they scorched his face and he dropped them! Down they fell, all the way to the bottom of Tall Tree with a CRASH!

His glasses were ruined! Smashed to pieces!

"Oh no!" wailed Terry in despair.

Grebby slithered over to the shattered spectacles, and picked up the pieces.

"Just leave this to me," he hissed and disappeared into the wilderness, in the direction of Big Water.

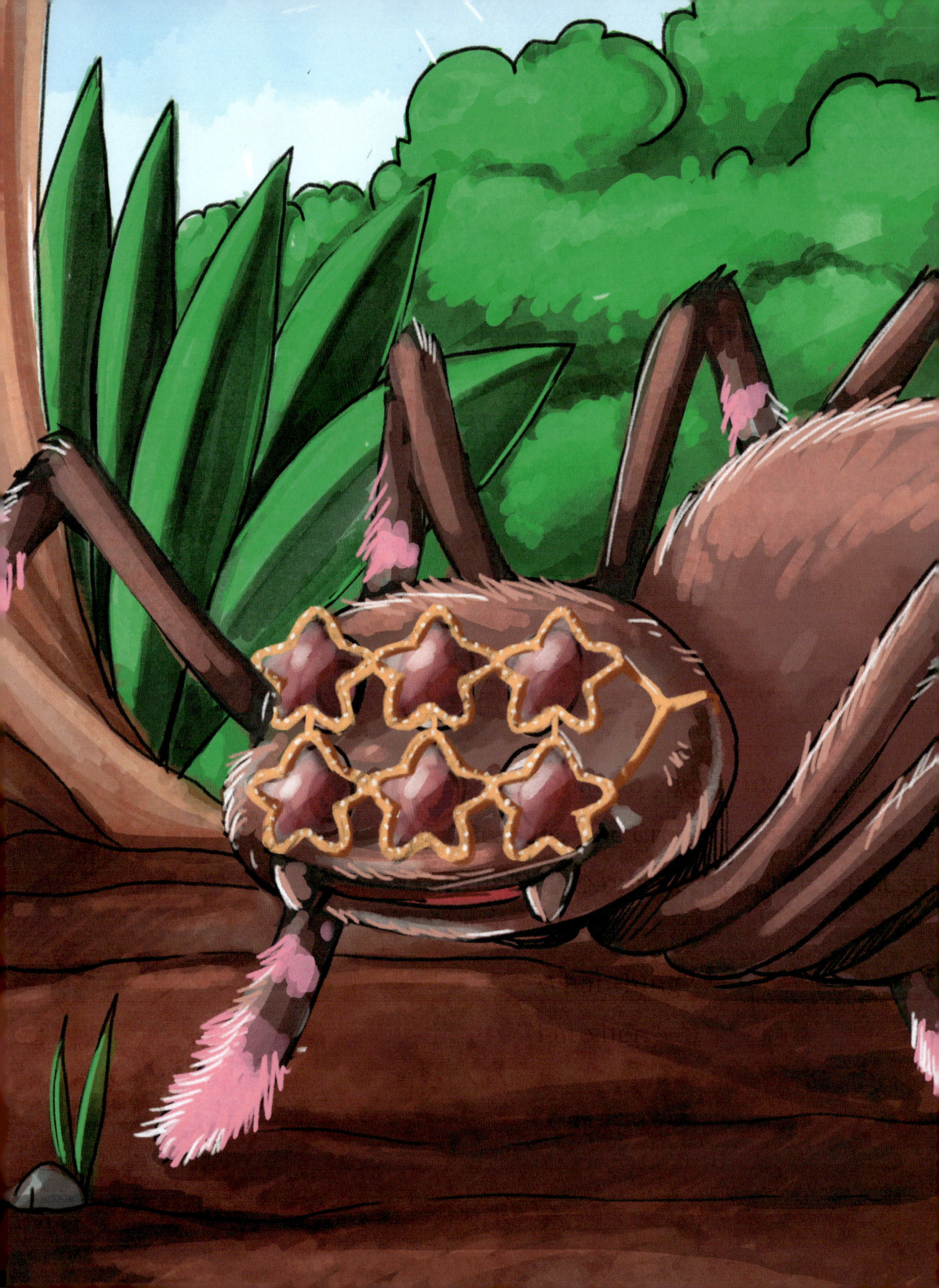

Grebby was gone a long time, the moon was high and full in the warm Brazilian sky by the time he finally returned carrying a small plastic case.

"Where have you been?" asked a curious Terry.

"Down to the surgery by Big Water," replied Grebby, "to get you some new glasses."

Terry felt ever so grateful, but then he remembered something, "But Grebby, what about you and Doc Croc?"

"Don't you worry about him," he grinned, a glint in his glassy green eyes, "let's just say I managed to persuade him."

"Oh," gulped Terry hoping that Grebby hadn't eaten poor old Doc Croc.

"Anyway, because you're a superstar I got you some superstar glasses," declared Grebby, opening the case to reveal some fantastic new glasses with each lens shaped like a star.

"Oh Grebby! Thanks!" gushed Terry, putting them on, "I love them!"

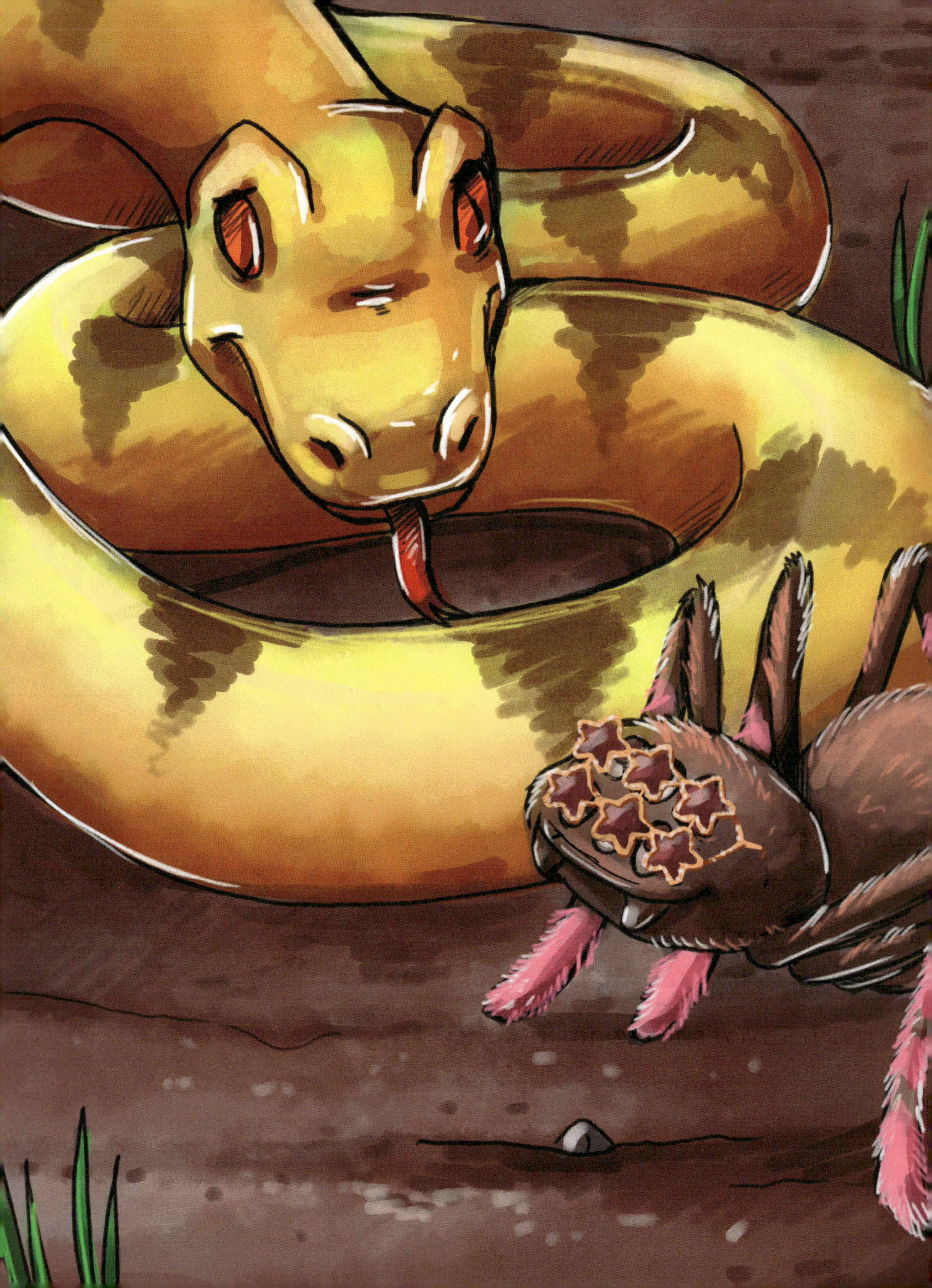

"You're welcome," smiled Grebby, "and listen, Terry, I'm sorry for teasing you and calling you Terry Twelve-Eyes, it was nasty of me."

"I forgive you, Grebby."

"It's no excuse, but I just wish I had legs like you."

"Well Grebby, I wish I had beautiful golden skin like you."

"Really? Well next time I shed my skin I'll be sure to save it for you!"

"Coolly-cool-cool!" grinned Terry.

And from that day to this, Grebby the Yellow Anaconda and Terry Tarantula have been the best of friends, and Grebby never called him Terry Twelve-Eyes ever again.

One day I shall tell you how Grebby managed to persuade Doc Croc, but the whisper around the rainforest is that Doc Croc is looking for a new monkey receptionist...

fin

# Would you like to meet Mark Shark? Scan the QR code below to listen along with Toby on YouTube...

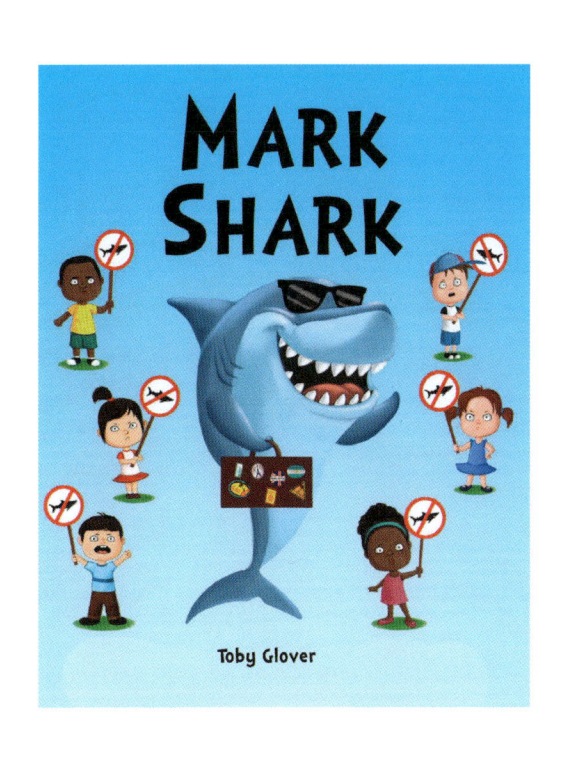

Printed in Great Britain
by Amazon